W9-ATO-859

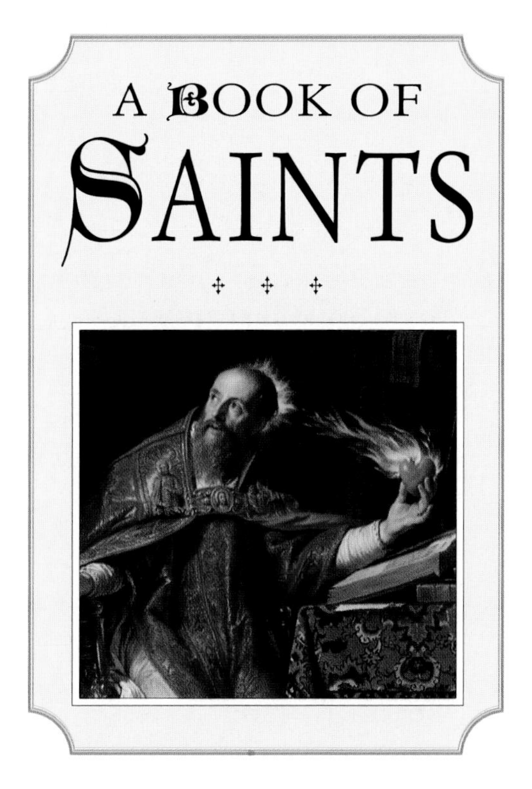
A BOOK OF
SAINTS

A BOOK OF SAINTS

✣ ✣ ✣

An evocative celebration in prose and paintings

This edition published in 1996 by
Smithmark Publishers, a division of U.S. Media Holdings, Inc.,
16 East 32nd Street,
New York,
NY 10016.

ISBN 0 8317 7311 1

Produced by Anness Publishing Limited
1 Boundary Row
London SE1 8HP

Printed in Singapore by Star Standard Industries Pte. Ltd.

10 9 8 7 6 5 4 3 2 1

CONTENTS

Chapter One
1st and 2nd Century
St John the Baptist 10
St Andrew 12
St Peter 13
St John the Evangelist 14
St Matthew 16
St Mary Magdalene 17
St Veronica 18
St Cecilia 19

Chapter Two
3rd to 5th Century
St Lawrence 22
St Margaret of Antioch 24
St George 26
St Christopher 27
St Catherine 28
St Paul the Hermit 29
St Martin of Tours 30
St Ambrose 32
St Nicholas 33
St Jerome 34
St Augustine of Hippo 36

Chapter Three
6th to 12th Century
St Patrick 40
St Geneviève 42
St Benedict 43
St David 44
St Bavo 45
St Bruno 46
St Thomas Becket 48

Chapter Four
13th to 20th Century
St Francis of Assisi 52
St Anthony of Padua 54
St Rock 55
St Joan of Arc 56
St Thomas More 58
St Ignatius of Loyola 60
St Bernadette 62
Mary MacKillop 63

Introduction

✣ ✣ ✣

For two thousand years Christians have drawn inspiration from the lives of the saints: the apostles and other disciples of Christ who mostly suffered martyrdom for their faith; the committed Christians who, in the centuries of persecution that followed, met similar fates with apparent equanimity or even enthusiasm; the great teachers and scholars, and founders of religious orders; those who renounced the world for a life of contemplation; and others – often quite simple souls – who struck a powerful chord by being chosen to witness miracles and visions.

Best loved of all the saints are probably those who are remembered for some picturesque story, often involving a single act of heroism or charity – St George and the dragon, St Martin and the beggar, St Jerome and the lion, St Nicholas and the children – however unverifiable the story may be historically. We will never know if Veronica did mop the face of Jesus on his agonizing journey with the cross, or whether George did slay the dragon, but we can tell the stories, and believe that they did.

Opposite: St Margaret of Antioch

Chapter One

✣ ✣ ✣

1st and 2nd Century

"But God hath chosen the foolish things of the world to confound the wise; and God hath chosen the weak things of the world to confound the things which are mighty."

1 Corinthians 1:27

Opposite: St Cecilia

St John the Baptist

Patron saint of motorways, of farriers and of the Knights Hospitallers

Feast day 24 June

✢ ✢ ✢

John the Baptist is said to have been the forerunner of the Messiah. Jesus said of him, "Among those that are born of women there is not a greater prophet." (Luke vii, 28) He was born to Elizabeth, cousin of the Virgin Mary.

John began preaching at the age of twenty-seven in the wilderness of Judaea. He lived an austere life, dressed in clothes made of camel hair and surviving on a diet of locusts and wild honey. He baptized those who came to listen to him and to confess their sins in the River Jordan. One day Jesus came to him for baptism, and although John was reluctant, having recognised Jesus as the saviour he was waiting for, the ceremony was carried out and the ministry of Jesus began.

John's public criticism of Herod Antipas for marrying his niece Herodias resulted in his imprisonment. Salome, Herodias's daughter, was promised any prize by Herod for her dancing. At her mother's behest she demanded the head of John the Baptist. Although Herod regretted his promise the execution was carried out.

Unusually the feast day of John the Baptist celebrates his birth rather than his death.

St Andrew

Patron saint of fishermen and of Scotland

Feast day 30 November

✣ ✣ ✣

Andrew, like his brother Simon, was a fisherman who lived at Capernaum on the Sea of Galilee. He was a disciple of John the Baptist and was with him at Bethany when he met Jesus and became the first of the apostles. After the arrest of John, Jesus came to Capernaum and, finding Andrew and Simon fishing, said, "Come and follow me. I will make you fishers of men."

Andrew later preached in various parts of Asia Minor, and after antagonizing the Roman governor of Achaia, in Greece, whose wife he had baptized, he was crucified at Patras in the year 60 – supposedly on an X-shaped cross. His relics, which were stolen from Constantinople during the Crusades, are likely to be those resting in the cathedral of Amalfi in Italy.

St Peter

Patron saint of the Church and of longevity

Feast day 29 June

✣ ✣ ✣

After being called with his brother Andrew to follow Jesus, this humble fisherman became his staunchest disciple. Originally named Simon, he was given the name of Peter, meaning the rock on which the Church was to be built.

He seems to have accompanied Jesus throughout his ministry, his loyalty and courage only wavering after the arrest of Jesus in the Garden of Gethsemane, when, as his master had predicted, he three times denied knowing him. After the Resurrection, however, it was to Peter that Jesus entrusted the care of the Church, exorting him to "feed my sheep".

Peter is believed to have preached the Gospel in Antioch before becoming the first Bishop of Rome. There he was crucified in the year 64, upside down at his own request, and was buried where St Peter's cathedral now stands.

St John the Evangelist

Patron saint of writers

Feast day 27 December

✣ ✣ ✣

John, born in Galilee, was a fisherman with his brother James when they were called to follow Jesus. Of all the apostles, only John, "the disciple whom Jesus loved", is recorded as having been present at the Crucifixion, and it was to him that Jesus entrusted the care of his mother Mary. He was also the first of the apostles to recognize Jesus after the Resurrection.

John escaped martyrdom, but only narrowly, for legend has it that he survived being thrown into a cauldron of boiling oil and later being forced to drink poison as a test of his faith.

As well as his epistles and the fourth Gospel, he is believed to be the author of the Book of Revelation. He eventually became Bishop of Ephesus and lived to be over a hundred. Scholars dispute whether John the Evangelist was the same person as John the Divine – the author of the Book of Revelation – but tradition says they were.

St Matthew

Patron saint of accountants and tax-collectors

Feast day 21 September

✣ ✣ ✣

Matthew the Levite was a surprising choice as a disciple of Jesus, for he worked at Capernaum as a publican or tax-collector on behalf of the Romans – a lucrative job which would have earned him the contempt of his fellow Jews. However, when criticized by the Pharisees for associating with such people, Jesus replied, "It is not those who are in health that have need of the physician; it is those who are sick."

Matthew's account of the Gospel was not only written first, between 60 and 90, but in Aramaic, the language used by Jesus himself. However, it only survives in a Greek translation.

"Matthew the publican", as he modestly refers to himself – though he seldom does at all – later preached the Gospel in Persia and Ethiopia, where he is said to have died a martyr's death.

St Mary Magdalene

Patron saint of penitant sinners and the contemplative life

Feast day 22 July

✣ ✣ ✣

Mary Magdalene was one of Jesus's most devoted disciples and was present at the Crucifixion. It was to Mary, weeping near the empty tomb where she had gone to anoint his body, that Jesus first revealed himself on Easter Day. In her confusion she thought at first he was the gardener, and asked where Jesus's body had been taken. Then, "with fear and great joy", she recognized him.

It used to be thought that this Mary – the fallen woman who anointed the feet of Jesus – and the Mary who was the sister of Martha and Lazarus were the same person.

A pleasant, if doubtful, tradition also has it that Mary Magdalene escaped persecution and ended her days in quiet seclusion in Provence, from where her body was removed at the time of the Moorish invasion to Vezelay in Burgundy.

ST VERONICA

PATRON SAINT OF WASHERWOMEN

FEAST DAY 12 JULY

✣ ✣ ✣

The story goes that when Jesus stumbled and fell while carrying his cross to Calvary, the saintly Veronica stepped forward and wiped his face with her veil. An impression of his features was left on the cloth, imbuing it with the power of healing. It is said that she once cured Tiberius, the Roman emperor.

Since the eighth century St Veronica's veil, or "the Veronica" has been among the relics at St Peter's in Rome. It has been suggested, admittedly, that as *vera icon* means true image, the relic may have given rise to the legend; if so, there are few more charming.

St Cecilia

Patron saint of musicians

Feast day 22 November

✥ ✥ ✥

Cecilia was a Roman martyr of patrician birth who dedicated her virginity to Christ. When she was married, against her will, to a non-Christian named Valerian, she sat apart, ignoring the festive wedding music, and "sang to the Lord in her heart". On their wedding night, she broke the news of her vow, and her husband, to his credit, agreed to respect it.

Indeed Valerian and his brother were both converted themselves, but were later executed for giving Christian burial to the bodies of martyrs. When Cecilia did the same for them, she too chose death rather than renounce her faith. Such was her dignity that hundreds of her accusers were converted, and the story of how she miraculously survived for three days after several bungled attempts to execute her, by suffocation and beheading, produced one of the most popular cults of the Middle Ages.

Chapter Two

✣ ✣ ✣

3rd to 5th Century

"We make ourselves a ladder out of our vices if we trample the vices themselves underfoot."

St Augustine of Hippo

Opposite: St Jerome

St Lawrence

Patron saint of cooks

Feast day 10 August

✢ ✢ ✢

A Spaniard by birth, Lawrence was a deacon of Rome under Pope Sixtus II. When the Pope was executed in 258 during the persecution of the Emperor Valerian, the distraught Lawrence was commanded by the prefect to hand over the treasure of the Church. His response was to assemble a large number of the city's poor, to whom he had distributed the wealth, and present them to the prefect. This, he said, was it. The prefect, infuriated, ordered a gridiron to be set up and Lawrence to be roasted until he revealed the whereabouts of the treasure.

Lawrence appears to have remained not only stoical during his ordeal but remarkably good-humoured. "I'm done on one side," he said at one point. "Won't you turn me over?" Lawrence died, uttering a prayer for the conversion of Rome.

St Margaret of Antioch

Patron saint of pregnant women

Feast day 20 July

✣ ✣ ✣

The legend of Margaret (or Marina) of Antioch may have little basis in fact but had a wide currency in the Middle Ages. She was said to be the daughter of a senior pagan priest, to whom she gave terminal offence by converting to Christianity and vowing to remain a virgin.

Banished from home, she became a shepherdess, only to attract the unwanted attentions of a prefect named Olybrius. Her lack of compliance led him to denounce her as a Christian, and she was subjected to a variety of tortures.

Margaret's faith sustained her in prison, however, and legend has it that the cross she wore saved her from being swallowed alive by Satan in the form of a dragon, in whose gullet it stuck. Finally she was beheaded, but as her cult spread, it became the custom in pregnancy to pray to her for a safe delivery.

St George

Patron saint of soldiers and of England

Feast day 23 April

✣ ✣ ✣

Although several legends exist, little is known for certain about St George except that he was a soldier who died for his faith in Palestine in about 303.

In the most familiar legend the knight errant came across a Libyan city whose inhabitants were being terrorized by a persistent dragon. The creature had to be appeased with flesh, and having already consumed all their sheep, it had started on the children, who were chosen by lot for sacrifice. George arrived just in time to save the king's daughter by fighting off the dragon and killing it with his lance. At this point thousands of relieved citizens were apparently baptized on the spot – though in one version of the legend the knight had made their conversion a precondition for his helping them. In the fourteenth century St George was made the patron saint of England, after appearing in a vision to crusaders in the Holy Land.

St Christopher

Patron saint of travellers

Feast day 25 July

✣ ✣ ✣

Little is known about the historical Christopher, who was martyred at Lycia in what is now Turkey, beyond the fact that he was immensely strong and could have escaped had he wished.

The Christopher of legend was a giant of a man called Reprobus who took on the job of carrying travellers across a river. One day he discovered that an exceptionally heavy burden had been the child Jesus, who gave him his new name, meaning bearer of Christ. His staff, which Jesus instructed him to plant in the ground, bore fruit the following day.

It was said that anyone looking on an image of St Christopher would come to no harm that day. This made him extremely popular, both with those setting out on a journey, and with the artists who depict him.

St Catherine

Patron saint of millers and wheelwrights

Feast day 25 November

✣ ✣ ✣

According to legend Catherine was an Alexandrian aristocrat of great beauty and learning – and she knew it. Having consented to be married only if her equal could be found, she received a visit from the Virgin Mary and the child Jesus. While Catherine was perfectly willing to marry Jesus, he rejected her for the ugliness of her soul. After she had embraced Christianity and learned humility, the visit was repeated and Jesus, now finding her beautiful, agreed to their "mystical marriage".

When Catherine declared her faith, the emperor Maxentius produced fifty philosophers to talk some sense into her. However, she defeated their arguments and they were converted instead – and executed. Finally Maxentius had the defiant Catherine thrust into a murderous contraption of wheels and blades – the inspiration of the catherine wheel firework.

St Paul the Hermit

Patron saint of weavers

Feast day 15 January

✣ ✣ ✣

The first known hermit, Paul, was an Egyptian who at the age of twenty-two, believing that he was about to be denounced as a Christian by his brother-in-law, fled into the Theban desert, where he remained for the next ninety years, praying and contemplating God.

He lived in a cave, dressed in the leaves of a palm tree which also provided his food, and seems to have been happy. After about twenty years, according to St Jerome, his biographer, Paul began to receive half a loaf of bread each day, delivered by a raven. When, at the age of about eighty, he was visited by another hermit, St Anthony, the bird even had the presence of mind, apparently, to increase this to a whole loaf.

Many years later St Anthony came again, only to find that his friend, who had appeared to be deep in prayer, had finally gone to meet his maker.

St Martin of Tours

Patron saint of beggars and of France

Feast day 11 November

This immensely popular saint, born in what is now Hungary in 316, began his career as a conscript in the Roman cavalry. Stationed at Amiens, in Gaul, he met a beggar in distress on a frosty night and promptly cut his own cloak in two and gave him half. He was rewarded with a vision of Christ wearing the cloak, and was later baptized.

Having left the army, Martin lived for ten years as a hermit monk, founding the first monastery in Gaul at Liguge, before being persuaded to accept the bishopric of Tours. He continued to live in the style of a monk, but performed the job energetically, travelling all over his diocese and beyond, preaching, healing and converting the heathen; opposing heresy, but advocating leniency towards heretics.

When Martin died in November 397, his coffin was followed by two thousand monks, and it is said that the trees came into leaf as it passed.

St Ambrose

Patron saint of beekeepers, of orators and of geese

Feast day 7 December

✣ ✣ ✣

When Auxentius, the bishop of Milan, died in 374, chaos resulted as the Catholics and Arians argued about who should succeed him. Ambrose, then the governor of Liguria and Aemilia, tried to calm the crowd. Above the tumult a voice – allegedly that of a child – cried out "Ambrose, bishop!" Ambrose was persuaded by the emperor Valentinian to accept the post on 7 December 374, at the age of thirty-five. Already well educated – he was a poet, orator and lawyer of note – Ambrose now applied himself to the study of the Scriptures and theology.

One of the best-loved bishops of the Church, Ambrose had enormous influence on the history of Western Christianity. He composed hymns, some of which survive today, and spoke in praise of the virtue of virginity, producing a popular treatise on the subject. Accused in some quarters with trying to depopulate the empire, he replied that wars, not maidens, are the destroyers of the human race.

St Nicholas

Patron saint of children, of sailors, merchants, pawnbrokers and of Russia

Feast day 6 December

✣ ✣ ✣

The man who gave rise to the Santa Claus legend is a shadowy but immensely popular saint whose fame rests on a few remarkable deeds he performed while he was Bishop of Myra, in what is now Turkey.

On hearing that three sisters, whose father could not afford dowries, were about to be made to earn them in a regrettable way, Nicholas saved their honour by anonymously donating three balls of gold. His patronage of children stems from his discovery, in a butcher's cellar, of three murdered boys, pickled in a barrel of brine, whom he miraculously restored to life. He also rescued three sailors from drowning, and three falsely accused prisoners from execution.

Although Nicholas is thought to have died by the time of the Council of Nicaea (Nice) in 325, some say that he was indeed there, and during a lively debate struck an opponent on the jaw to emphasize a point. His remains are in Bari, Italy.

St Jerome

Patron saint of students and librarians

Feast day 30 September

✣ ✣ ✣

If Jerome's abrasive personality made him something of a borderline case as a saint, his prodigious intellect made him one of the foremost teachers and scholars in the history of the Church.

Born in Dalmatia in about 347, Jerome was brought up as a Christian but was already about thirty, and widely travelled, when he became a monk. He then had a four-year spell in the Syrian desert, living as a hermit and studying the scriptures. There he is said to have removed a thorn from the paw of a lion, which became his faithful friend.

Jerome was ordained in Antioch and then became secretary to Pope Damasus I in Rome, where he began his greatest work of biblical scholarship, the accurate and accessible Latin translation that became known as the Vulgate. In 386 he travelled to Bethlehem, where he founded a monastery and remained until his death in about 420.

St Augustine of Hippo

Patron saint of theologians

Feast day 28 May

✣ ✣ ✣

Augustine was born in Tagaste, in what is now Algeria, in 354. He was a great disappointment to his mother, Monica, because from the age of sixteen he lived in sin with an older woman; he espoused the doctrine of Manichaeism; and taught rhetoric in Carthage and later in Milan.

However, after rediscovering his faith and being baptized by St Ambrose in 387, Augustine returned to Africa, founded a monastery and in 396 was appointed Bishop of Hippo. He became one of the greatest of all Christian thinkers, and for thirty-five years preached and wrote tirelessly against all forms of heresy.

He died in 430, as the Vandals were on the point of sacking Hippo. Fortunately his autobiograpy *Confessions*, which, like *The City of God,* reveal the brilliance of his intellect, survived for posterity, together with his famous prayer: "Give me chastity and continence, O Lord, but not yet".

VERÍTAS

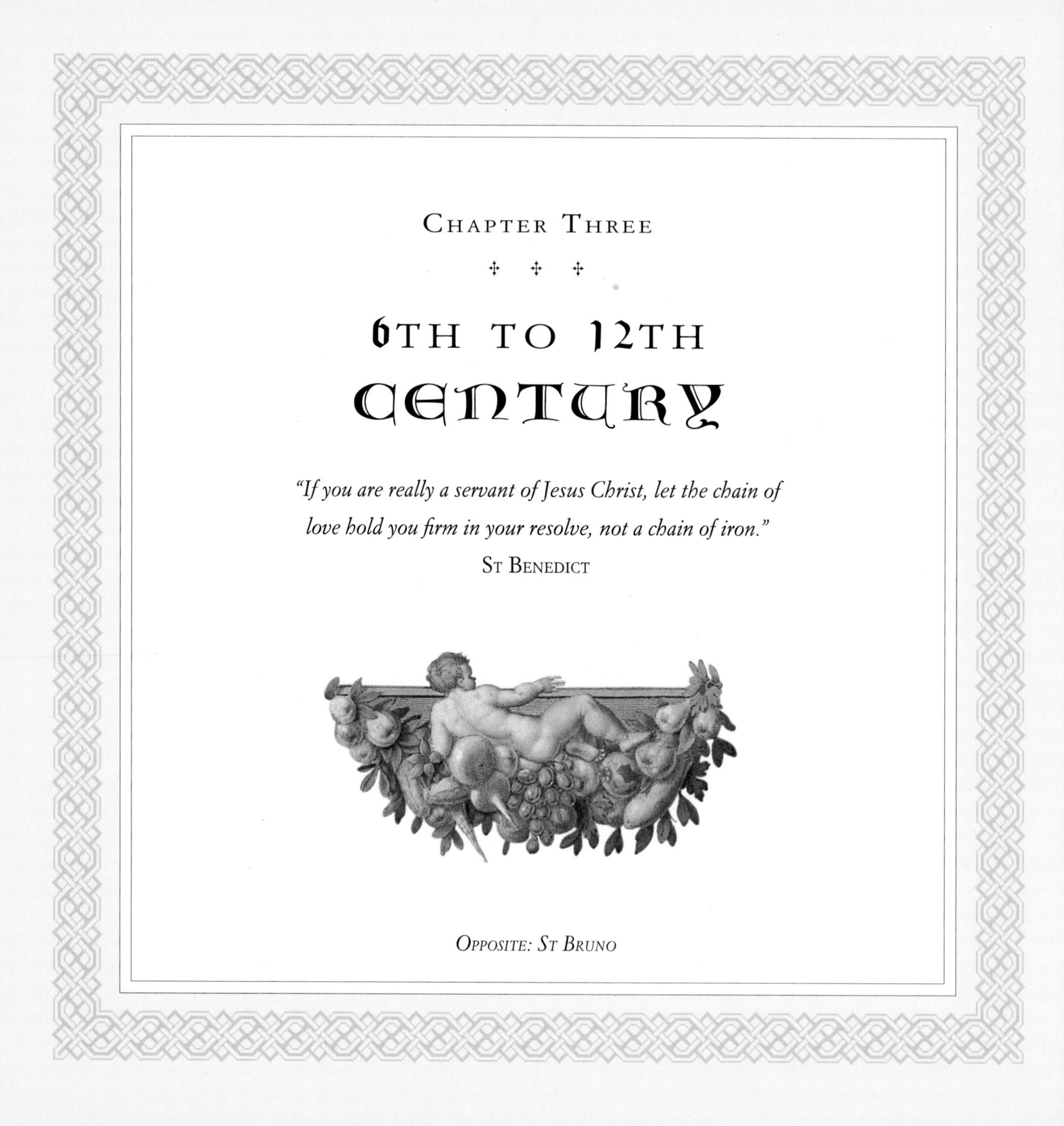

CHAPTER THREE

6TH TO 12TH CENTURY

"If you are really a servant of Jesus Christ, let the chain of love hold you firm in your resolve, not a chain of iron."

ST BENEDICT

OPPOSITE: ST BRUNO

St Patrick

Patron saint of Ireland

Feast day 17 March

✣ ✣ ✣

It is thought that Patrick was born in the west of Britain in about 389 and was the son of a Roman official. He was captured by Picts while still a boy and sold as a slave in Ireland, but after about six years' work as a herdsman he escaped on a ship bound for Gaul. Already religious, he became a disciple of St Germanus of Auxerre, who later consecrated him as a bishop.

In 432 Patrick returned to Ireland as a missionary. In spite of opposition he succeeded in converting chiefs and whole tribes, and founded churches and monasteries, first in the north, then throughout the country. He is said to have performed many miracles, most famously expelling all the snakes from Ireland. He died in about 460 at Saul, on Strangford Lough in County Down.

St Geneviève

Patron saint of Paris

Feast day 3 January

✣ ✣ ✣

Geneviève was born in Nanterre in about 420, and may have been a shepherdess before becoming a nun at the age of fifteen and moving to Paris.

During the siege of Paris by the Franks, Geneviève not only led a bold expedition to bring back food, but persuaded the Frankish king, Childeric, to release prisoners. Later, when Attila's Huns threatened to attack Paris, they left it unscathed, and it was widely believed that Geneviève's prayers had saved the city.

Although the Franks had succeeded in taking Paris, their next king, Clovis, was converted to Christianity, and when she died, Geneviève was buried in the church he had founded. She is said to watch over the city, and miraculous escapes from disaster are widely held to be due to her intercession.

St Benedict

Patron saint of schoolchildren and of Europe

Feast day 21 March

✣ ✣ ✣

The lovable Benedict was born in Nursia in about 480, and as a young man was sent to study in Rome. He was so shocked by the sinful life of the city that he went off to be a hermit in the mountains of Subiaco, where it is said his food was lowered to him in a basket.

A spell as a somewhat strict abbot ended with an attempt to poison him, which he miraculously foiled by blessing the fatal cup, which broke. Returning to the mountains, he set up twelve small monasteries, where he led by example.

Later he installed his followers at Monte Cassino, replacing a pagan temple on the hilltop with a great abbey. Here he formulated the Rule of Saint Benedict, based on moderation, obedience, kindness and respect, which, although never intended to be a general prescription, nevertheless set the pattern for monastic life throughout the Western Christian world.

St David

Patron saint of Wales

Feast day 1 March

✢ ✢ ✢

The son of a Welsh chieftain, David studied the scriptures for ten years under St Paulinus, a scribe, whose eyesight he miraculously restored. He then took to missionary work, and founded twelve monasteries, including Glastonbury, before eventually becoming Archbishop of Wales.

At David's own monastery at Mynyw, discipline was the watchword: continuous praying from dusk on Friday till dawn on Sunday; cold baths; no help from oxen in tilling the fields; no meat or fish to eat – they lived on bread, leeks and water – and no talking except in emergency.

Surprisingly, David himself was an eloquent speaker, who won the argument convincingly at the Synod of Brefi. There, it is said, the ground swelled up beneath his feet so that he could be seen, while a white dove on his shoulder allowed all to hear him – just two of many miracles attributed to David.

St Bavo

Patron saint of Ghent

Feast day 1 October

✣ ✣ ✣

Bavo was a nobleman in Brabant, in the Low Countries, who on realizing what a corrupt and selfish life he had led, underwent a dramatic conversion. He repented of his heartless treatment of others, and proceeded to give away all his wealth and property. When he happened to meet a man whom he had once sold into serfdom, he insisted on the humiliation of being led on the end of a chain as a penance.

On one of his estates, near Ghent, St Amand built a monastery, which Bavo was allowed to enter. The monastic life, however, was not austere enough for the convert and he obtained permission to live as a hermit. For a while a hollow tree was his home; later a tiny hut in a forest, where he died in 633.

St Bruno

Founder of the Carthusian Order

Feast day 6 October

✣ ✣ ✣

Bruno was born in Cologne in 1030 and studied at Rheims, where he rose to a high position in the university and Church. After helping to denounce his corrupt archbishop, Manasses, Bruno was banished for his trouble, but was able to return to Rheims when Manasses was excommunicated.

However, Bruno had conceived the idea of a new order of monks, who would live like the hermits of old. In 1084 he and six companions moved to La Grande Chartreuse, a remote spot in the mountains near Grenoble, to begin their simple, austere existence composed of worship, penitance, hard manual work and the copying of manuscripts.

In 1090 Bruno was summoned to Italy to be an advisor to the Pope. Life in Rome was not to his taste, and he was allowed to live in another "charterhouse" in the mountains of Calabria. Here he remained in tranquil contentment until his death in 1101.

St Thomas Becket

Saint invoked against blindness

Feast day 29 December

✢ ✢ ✢

Thomas Becket, the wealthy and flamboyant archdeacon of Canterbury, was not yet forty when Henry II appointed him chancellor of England. He was highly regarded by his king, but when he was also appointed Archbishop of Canterbury he embraced austerity and infuriated Henry, first by resigning as chancellor and then by putting Church before State and siding with the Pope against the King. Forced to flee to France, he remained there six years before being forgiven and returning to Canterbury.

Further quarrels soon ensued, until in 1170 Henry famously exclaimed, "Who will rid me of this turbulent priest!" Four knights, eager to please, took him at his word, entered Canterbury cathedral and murdered Thomas. Shock waves went round the Christian world, Thomas was canonized three years later, Henry performed public penance, and for centuries to come pilgrims flocked to Thomas's shrine.

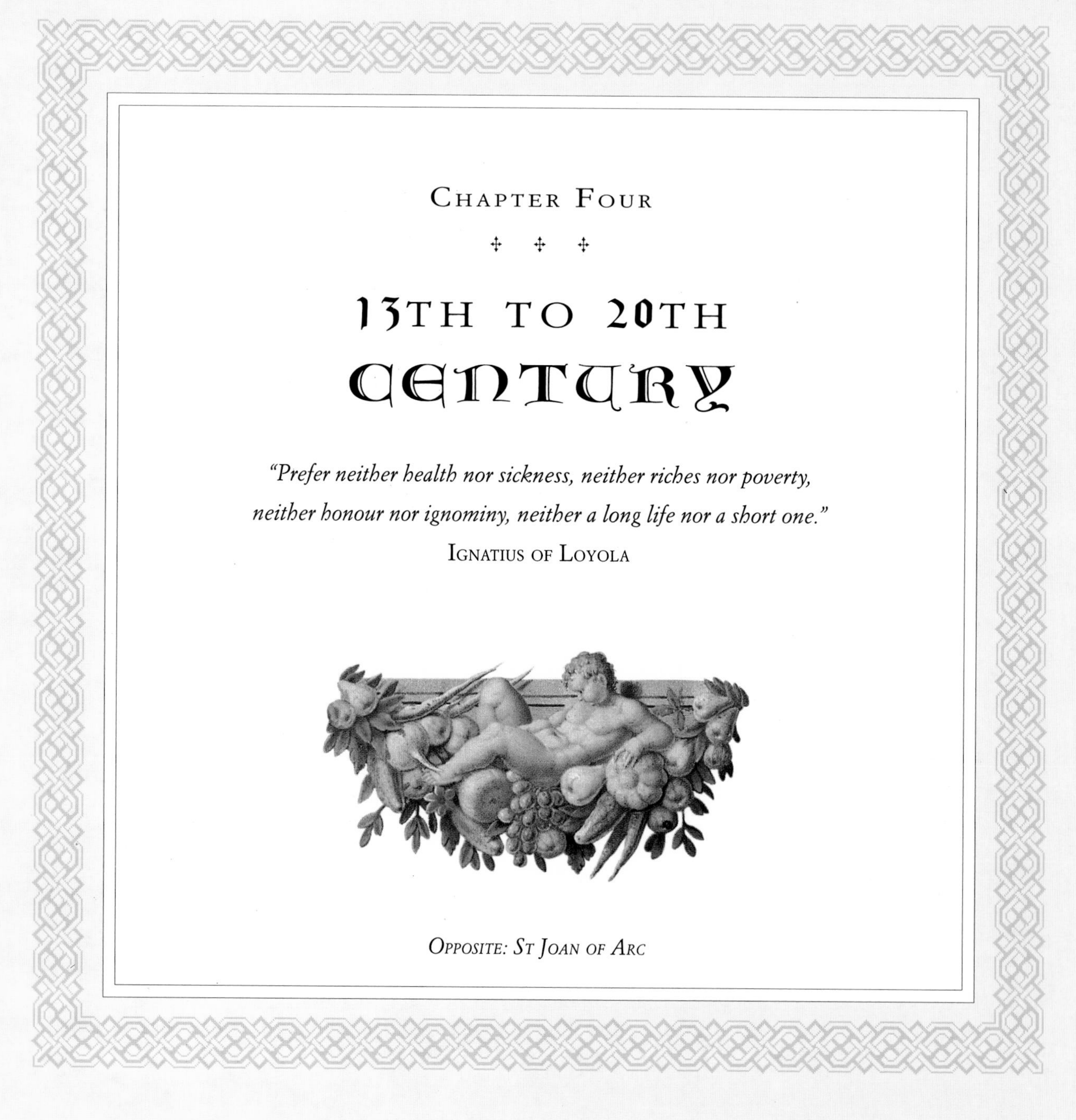

Chapter Four

✣ ✣ ✣

13th to 20th Century

"Prefer neither health nor sickness, neither riches nor poverty, neither honour nor ignominy, neither a long life nor a short one."

Ignatius of Loyola

Opposite: St Joan of Arc

St Francis of Assisi

Patron saint of animals and of Italy

Feast day 4 October

✣ ✣ ✣

Born in Assisi in 1181, Francis was the only son of a wealthy merchant. As a young man he was an extravagant, fun-loving character, but while returning home after a spell of soldiering he had an experience which changed his life. Meeting a leper on the road, he suddenly felt impelled to overcome his revulsion and kiss the man's hand. Thereafter he renounced home and property for a wandering life of teaching and prayer.

Francis soon attracted followers and in 1209 founded the Franciscan Order of Friars Minor, "little brothers", who took vows of poverty, chastity and obedience. His own humble life exemplified the love of God, while his unique rapport with the animal kingdom, famously illustrated by his sermon to the birds and his taming of the wolf of Gubbio, has made him perhaps the most popular of all the saints.

He died in 1226, having borne Christ's stigmata for two years, and was canonized in 1228.

St Anthony of Padua

Patron saint of the poor and of Portugal

Feast day 13 June

✣ ✣ ✣

This little Portuguese friar was a brilliant preacher, whose fiery sermons in the open air drew enormous crowds. His attacks on usury and greed especially endeared him to the poor.

Born in Lisbon, he joined the Augustinians, but later left to become a Franciscan. He was sent to preach to the heathen in North Africa, but fell ill and had to return to Assisi. Instead St Francis dispatched him to teach in Padua. He also taught at universities in southern France, where he preached forcefully against the Albigensian heresy.

Anthony died at the age of thirty-six, having won a reputation as a miracle worker and leaving a wealth of popular legends. On one occasion a novice monk who had borrowed his prayerbook without asking returned it hastily after seeing a terrifying apparition. Anthony is regularly invoked to find lost belongings, and is also patron saint of the lower animals, which is why he is sometimes depicted with a donkey.

St Rock

Patron saint of plague victims

Feast day 16 August

✢ ✢ ✢

Rock was born in Montpellier, where his father was governor. When, at the age of twenty, he lost both his parents and inherited a fortune, Rock gave it all away to the poor and set off on a pilgrimage to Rome. There he became famous for nursing those sick with the plague, many of whom were miraculously cured. When Rock himself caught the plague, he went off into a forest, where a faithful dog not only brought him bread each day but licked his sores till he recovered.

Disappointment awaited him on his return to Montpellier. He had become so thin that no one recognized him, and he was thrown into prison as an imposter. Only after his death was a distinctive birthmark discovered which proved his identity. Fifty years later he was canonized, after his intercession was believed to have ended another outbreak of the plague.

St Joan of Arc

Patron saint of soldiers and of France

Feast day 30 May

✣ ✣ ✣

In 1426, when the Hundred Years War was in its ninetieth year, a French farm girl named Joan began hearing the voices of three saints, instructing her to lead the French forces. Having made an uncannily accurate prophesy, Joan was granted an audience with the Dauphin, Charles. To test her, he disguised himself, but she instantly picked him out. This was accepted as proof of her divine inspiration, and, in spite of her age and gender, she was put at the head of the French army.

Clad in white armour, Joan won great victories, and Charles was duly crowned at Rheims. When she was captured by the Burgundians, however, he did nothing to help her, and she was handed over to the English. They conspired with the Bishop of Beauvais to put her on trial for heresy, and for wearing men's clothes. She was found guilty, to no one's surprise, and burnt at the stake in Rouen. One of the most inspiring and symbolic figures in history, the Maid of Orleans was finally canonized in 1920.

St Thomas More

Patron saint of lawyers

Feast day 22 June

✣ ✣ ✣

As well as being a distinguished lawyer and politician, Thomas More was a man of high integrity and powerful faith. From about 1516, the year in which his Utopia was published, he was seen as a prospect for high office, and in 1529 Henry VIII appointed him lord chancellor in succession to Wolsey.

The king had misjudged his man, however, for the two were soon at loggerheads. Thomas could not accept Henry's assumption of authority as head of the Church; nor could he sanction his "divorce" of Katharine of Aragon. He resigned and went home to Chelsea, defiantly refusing to sign the Act of Succession which rejected the authority of the Pope.

Thomas was uncompromising and, when found guilty of treason, went to the scaffold declaring himself to be "the king's good servant, but God's first".

St Ignatius of Loyola

Founder of the Jesuit Order

Feast day 31 July

✣ ✣ ✣

Ignatius was a swaggering, redheaded Spanish nobleman and a soldier by profession. Badly wounded at the siege of Pamplona, he underwent a long period of convalescence during which he read about the saints and discovered his vocation. He retired to Manresa to contemplate, made a pilgrimage to the Holy Land and then went to Paris to study.

In about 1534 Ignatius and six others took holy orders and founded the Society of Jesus. The aim of the Jesuits was, quite simply, the greater glory of God. They offered their obedient service to Pope Paul III, and in 1540 he approved the Society. Thereafter and until his death in 1556, Ignatius lived in Rome, directing his "spiritual soldiers" as they set up missions in parts of Africa, India, South America and the Far East.

AD
MAIOREMD
GLORIAM
QVICVNQVEH
IESV CHRIST

St Bernadette

Patron saint of shepherds

Feast day 18 February

✣ ✣ ✣

In 1858, near Lourdes, in the south-west of France, a simple, delicate shepherdess named Marie Bernadette Soubirous was collecting firewood by the River Gave when a vision of the Virgin Mary appeared to her. Nobody believed her, of course, but she went on to experience eighteen such visions, in one of which Mary revealed a spring and told the girl to drink from it. In a later vision she was instructed to build a chapel there.

Under rigorous questioning Bernadette stuck to her story and eventually it was accepted, especially when the spring appeared to have healing properties. Lourdes is now one of the most popular places of pilgrimage in the world, and there have been numerous reports of miraculous cures.

The humble Bernadette was alarmed by all the publicity and shunned it, eventually entering the convent of Notre Dame at Nevers where, ever frail, she died in 1879 at the age of thirty-five.

Mary MacKillop

Founder of the Sisters of St Joseph of the Sacred Heart

Feast day 8 August

✣ ✣ ✣

Mary MacKillop (1842–1909) dedicated her life to extending God's love and care to those in need. In 1995 Pope John Paul II acknowledged her goodness by bestowing the title "Blessed" upon her at the beatification ceremony in Sydney, Australia, making her "Australia's first saint".

At the age of twenty-four, Mary co-founded the Sisters of St Joseph of the Sacred Heart in South Australia with Julian Tenison Woods. Dedicated to providing free education to all who needed it, particularly to those in remote rural areas, the Order spread rapidly throughout Australia, and to New Zealand, with Sisters living among the people who needed them.

Mary remained a woman of deep faith, vision, compassion and courage throughout her life. Her strong conviction that God would provide, and her typical Australian perseverence, offer an inspiration for others. It is envisaged that before long Mary will be officially recognized throughout the world as a saint.

ACKNOWLEDGEMENTS

The following pictures are reproduced with kind permission of the Visual Arts Library, London:
p10: St John the Baptist (detail), 1505–16 by Grünewald, Colmar, Unterlinden. p14: St John, 15th cent, Berlin, Gemäldegalerie. p16: St Matthew and the Angel, 1602 by Caravaggio, Rome, San Luigi dei Francesi. p17: St Magdalen and St Catherine, 1445 by Witz, Strasbourg, Musée Notre-Dame. p18: St Veronica c1420, Master of Veronika, Munich, Alte Pinakothek, Edimedia. p19: St Cecilia playing a viola by Zampieri, 17th cent, Edimedia. p22: Martyrdom of St Lawrence by Tiziano, Madrid, Escorial, Edimedia. p23: St Lawrence on the throne by Domingo Ram and studio, Edimedia. p24: St Marguerite, 19th cent, anon, Edimedia. p25: St Marguerite d'Antioche by Coccapani, Edimedia. p26(left): St George, 16th cent, Venice, Accademia. p26(right): St George and the Dragon, 1460 by Uccello, London, National Gallery. p27: St Christopher, 15th cent, by Witz, Basel, Kunstmuseum. p28: The Mystic Marriage of St Catherine, 1527–31 by Parmigianino, London, National Gallery. p30: The Dream of St Martin, 14th cent, Assisi, St Francis Basilica. p31: St Louis, Morlaix, Church of St Martin, Edimedia. p32: Altarpiece of St Ambrose, 15th cent by Vivarini, Venice, S Maria dei Frari. p33: St Nicolas, Les Briards Church, Edimedia. p34: St Jerome in the desert, 1715 by Crespi, London, National Gallery. p36: St Augustine and St Monica, Edimedia. p37: St Augustine, 1660 by Champaigne, Los Angeles County Museum. p39: St Bruno, c1650 by Le Sueur, Edimedia. p40: St Patrick, 19th cent, Mary Evans Picture Library. p41: St Patrick and St Winifred, 1926 by Dearle, St Mary's Church, Thame/S Halliday. p42: St Genevieve in the Forest by Richter, Hamburg, Kunsthalle, Edimedia. p43: St Benedict, 14th cent attrib to Di Cione, Lisbon, Gulbenkian Foundation, Edimedia. p44: St David, late 15th cent, Hasting Hours, British Library.

The Bridgeman Art Library, London:
front jacket: Maesta: Detail of Saints including St John the Baptist, 1308–11 by Duccio di Buoninsegna, Museo dell'Opera del Duomo, Siena. back jacket: St John the Baptist and Saints by Cima da Conegliano, Giovanni Battista, Madonna dell'Orto, Venice. p2: St Jerome and the Angels by Guido Reni, Detroit Institute of Arts, Michegan. p7: St Margaret of Antioch by Charles Joseph Natoire, Phillips, The International Fine Art Auctioneers. p11: St John the Baptist in Meditation by Hieronymus Bosch, Museo Lazaro Galdiano, Madrid. p12: The Martyrdom of St Andrew by Jusepe Ribera, Museum of Fine Arts, Budapest. p13: St Peter by William Holman Hunt, Private Collection. p15: St John the Evangelist by Domenichino, II (Domenico Zampieri), Glynde Place, Sussex. p20: St Jerome and the Lion in the Monastery by Vittore Carpaccio, Scuola di San Giorgio degli Schiavoni, Venice. p29: St Paul the Hermit by Jusepe Ribera, Prado, Madrid. p35: St Jerome by French School, 17th cent, Agnew & Sons, London. p49: Scene from the Life of St Thomas a Becket, c1220, Trinity Chapel Windows, Canterbury Cathedral, Private Collection. p51: Joan of Arc's Entry into Orleans, 8th May 1429 by Henry Scheffer, Chateau de Versailles, France, Giraudon. p56: Joan of Arc at the Coronation of King Charles VII 1422, 1854 by Jean-Auguste Dominique Ingres, Louvre, Paris, Lauros-Giraudon. p57: Joan of Arc kissing the Sword of Deliverance, 1863 by Dante Gabriel Rossetti, Private Collection. p61: Saint Ignatius of Loyola, Founder of the Jesuits by Peter Paul Rubens, Musee de Sibiu, Rumania, Giraudon.